ORGANIZED
CHaos

by Sylvia Jessy

For workshops and support groups, please contact Sylvia Jessy for group discounts and additional materials.

ISBN 0-9664199-0-1

Edited by Teresa K. Flatley, WriteStyle
Illustrations by Jill Fromelius
Printed in the United States of America

CONTENTS

SECTION 2
TOOLS FOR CHANGE

SECTION 3

IDEAS FOR SPECIFIC AREAS

SECTION 4

SIMPLIFY AND LIVE YOUR LIFE

FORWARD

Organizing comes naturally to me. So naturally, in fact, that it took a while to realize that others were not able to tap into their natural organizing abilities. Thus, began my quest. I wanted to know why.

I started by observing all the rituals people are tied to and how some people choose to use passive-aggressive actions in an attempt to communicate their needs. Then I started observing how people back themselves into corners and react through lashing out, avoidance, illness or depression. I also observed that when these same people found a motivation strong enough to make them move, they were able to pull within and find their natural organizing abilities.

Many people feel caught in a situation (or life) that has no options. In that case, they would not want to be organized, or have more time, energy or space. Because then they would have to look squarely at their situation (or life) and make changes or decisions. Some people feel it's better to ignore the situation and just try to make it through this life.

I then started studying psychology, feng shui, avoidance techniques, abuse, different relations, and different philosophies. The common thread, to me, was that each of us has our own answers -- within. Once I came to that conclusion, I started researching how the self-help and organizing books were treating the subject. I discovered that many of the early ones were locked into:

DO WHAT I SAY
AND YOU WILL BE FINE.

Some of the more recent self-help books have changed to:
LOOK WITHIN.
THE ANSWERS ARE THERE.

HERE ARE SOME WAYS THAT MAY HELP YOU FIND THEM.

I then turned to my six years' worth of clients to see how they use the material I teach. I had observed very early in my search that people fall into some distinct categories – which are discussed in this book at length. I then observed that once my clients had this information and were able to go within and find their motivation, they were able to start making changes in their lives.

My hope is that you will take the information contained in this book and decide whether it works for you.

Good luck on the organizing journey!

OVERVIEW: THE KEY TO ORGANIZING

So you've spent your life thus far being unfairly told you're wrong, lazy, crazy or just plain stupid because you're not organized. And you've probably heard all the promises that "If you just use my structure, my product, my knowledge, my system...then you will be organized."

You don't have to listen to others anymore. The key to being organized is understanding yourself -- how you think and react; what are your obstacles, gifts and shortcomings.

Then you can learn to enhance your strengths and compensate for your weaknesses; to focus on your successes, not your failures. You may even come up with a different definition of failure.

This book is a guide based on the premise that to be organized, you must first understand yourself. The most important piece of the organizing equation is YOU. Everything else is just "stuff."

Together, we will explore where you are now, the tools you need for change and how to keep the process going.

This book is designed to be read in sections. The first section deals with where you are. It's important that you recognize yourself as someone who wants to tap into his/her own organizing abilities before we start talking about how to change. Change starts the moment we really accept who and where we are. Until then, we are in denial and avoidance.

Self-awareness is the first step to self-change. Reading this book will allow you to recognize your natural organizing abilities and how you may have been sabotaging your life.

The second section deals with the tools you will need to implement the changes needed to become organized. Information is given by organizing style, and by problem areas.

The third section deals with specific areas you may need to organize in your home and office.

The fourth section deals with maintaining the organizing program and watching that you don't fall into old patterns.

You will find information in this book that will change your life -- if you are ready for change. This book will **not** tell you what to do; it will offer suggestions. It will tell stories of how others have changed their lives. It will offer a way out of the life you don't want.

Do not take the information in this book as YOUR answers. I wish for you to go within and determine your own answers. This book will help you find your way.

If you are ready for change, turn the page.

SECTION 1

WHERE

YOU ARE

NOW

CHAPTER 1

WHAT DOES IT MEAN TO
BE ORGANIZED?

What does "being organized" mean? Does it
look a certain way? Does it use particular tools?
How does it work and how can we capture this
enigma?

For Organized Chaos, being organized
means being able to **find what we need – when we
need it** – with the least amount of work involved.

Obsessive-Compulsive or "Oscar Madison"
types might say, "That's not enough. It's got to
look and be perfect."

Messies or "Felix Unger" types might say, "That will take way too long. I'd rather go and play."

"Being organized" is not something that takes a long time to achieve. Decluttering the piles or rooms we've junked up, however, may take a lot longer. But remember they didn't get junked up overnight.

"Being organized" is a behavior modification best achieved by small incremental steps. Suppose, for example, that you've not been able to easily locate your keys when you're ready to leave your home or office. A simple solution would be to set up a staging area today. A staging area is simply an area designated to house stuff on its way into your house/office or on its way out. You have now achieved "being organized" in one small area.

This is how most change occurs in our lives -- in small bits. We didn't end up overwhelmed in one day. But in one day we can start to make changes that will affect us on every level.

It's 8 a.m. Do you know where your keys are? Of course you do. They're in the staging area you created yesterday.

CHAPTER 2

WHAT IS CHAOS?

Chaos is that place from which our creativity comes. It is also creativity run amuck.

"Before the beginning of great brilliance, there must be chaos."

I Ching

When you look at your environment, do you see opportunity or obstacles? The difference between these two is that opportunities can allow us to be passionate about doing something while moving us closer to our goals.

Obstacles, on the other hand, are standing in the way of achieving our goals. Obstacles can be opportunities run amuck.

When planting a garden, you plant the seeds and water and fertilize them, waiting till the plants come up. If the plants come up too closely together, even if they are healthy, they cannot all live.

The same is true of opportunities. If you keep all the opportunities and try to let them all grow or simply hold them till later, there is no room for all of them to survive.

Just as we need space and time to grow, so do our opportunities.

By holding onto multiple opportunities (i.e. articles that will be perfect for us if we could get around to reading them, unfinished projects, books that are not relevant in the moment, clothes that don't fit), we are turning opportunities into obstacles. By allowing ourselves to let go of some of the opportunities, we can allow ourselves to focus on the opportunities in front of us and give them the time, space and energy to grow.

Harness your chaos and put it to work for you.

CHAPTER 3

I'M RIGHT!
NO, I'M RIGHT!
WHICH ORGANIZING
STYLE IS RIGHT?

Visual vs. Camouflager. Sounds a lot like something right out of a war movie. But even though organization isn't actually about war (or at least not when it is done effectively), people have been engaged in battles and skirmishes for decades about the proper way to organize their "stuff."

It is important to keep Organized Chaos' definition of being organized in mind. Being organized is being able to find what we need when we need it. When you were growing up, however, do you remember hearing things like: "My way is right, your way is wrong" or "You're just too lazy to do it the right way?"

Each of us is born with a unique organizing style. Unfortunately, most people don't accept these individual differences and think their way of organizing is the only way to organize. So parents, peers, teachers and other very well-intentioned people have tried to show us the "right" way (a.k.a. their way) of organizing.

Secretary talking to co-worker, "I can't find my boss."

Co-worker smiles and says, "Keep looking, he's behind the piles on his desk."

This has produced several myths about organization:

- We are not good enough because we can't be organized like everyone else.
- Everyone else is organized.
- Being organized means things have to look a certain way.

Let's consider the different organizing styles we are born with. Look at the Organizing Style Line on the next page. On one end of the line you see the word "Visual;" on the other, the word "Camouflager."

Review the descriptions to determine your unique style. After reviewing the descriptions, you may find it simple to recognize your style. Keep in mind, however, that your style may not be so extreme or you may be a combination of the two styles. If you need a little help in deciding, read the first line under Visual and the first line under Camouflager, then mark the "Organizing Style Line" closest to the description that represents you. Then move to the next line. After you have completed them all, your style should be evident by the most marks in one area.

If you're still not sure, check the end of this chapter to see illustrations of an unorganized Visual's and Camouflager's office.

VISUAL	CAMOUFLAGER
Wants everything out in the open	Wants everything out of sight
Piles of papers everywhere	Clear, clean desk
Drawers left open	Closed drawers
Closet doors left open	Closet doors closed
Floor or chairs used as desks	Clear floor and chairs
Items placed on floor as reminders	Things stuffed under desk
Tops removed from stuffed boxes	Things stuffed in boxes with lids

There is no right or wrong answer, just the one that best represents your true style. Once we understand our own unique style of organizing we can begin the organizing process "our way."

Illustration of an unorganized Visual's Office

See how things are in sight.

Illustration of an unorganized Camouflager's Office

See how things are hidden.

CHAPTER 4

WORK STYLES – ARE THEY INNATE OR LEARNED?

Just as each of us is born with a unique organizing style, each of us is also born with a unique working style.

There are two distinct working styles. Please review the descriptions to determine your natural way of working. Remember, we can train ourselves to work in either working style, but your natural style is the one with which you are most comfortable.

You may be using different styles in different environments. Some find they are Focused at work, but at home they are Grazers. This may be caused by external influences. (Examples: At work, you may have no choice over the furniture you use. At work, you may be Focused, but at home you cannot work that way.)

GRAZER	FOCUSED
Works on multiple projects simultaneously	Focuses on one project at a time
Needs to have several projects pending	Needs to ignore the pending projects
Gets a rush from the excitement of having lots of projects in process	Gets drained from the excitement & drama of too much going on
Gets bored by the same daily grind	Gets energized by following a lead through to completion

Understanding your natural way of working will aid you in setting up your environment to be most conducive to your productivity.

"Why does my boss have to keep interrupting me every ten minutes? Amy, the secretary, wailed to the organizer. "Can't he see that I'm busy?"

The organized asked, "When we had the workshop yesterday, which natural style of working described you best?"

"Focused, definitely. But, what's that got to do with him interrupting me?," asked Amy.

"Focused workers prefer to focus on their work at hand and can get irritated by constant interruptions," the organizer explained.

"That's it exactly. But what can I do? I'm only a secretary."

"What if your boss agrees to have a pre-set meeting with you twice a day to give you work and not interrupt you unless it's an emergency? Would that help?"

"That's a great idea. That means I can focus on my work and get it done in half the time it's taking now. What a solution!," Amy said.

CHAPTER 5

RECOGNIZING SHOULDS

In order to really begin the process of
decluttering, organizing and simplifying, we first
need to recognize those thoughts and ideas which
keep us from moving forward. An example of this
would be: "I can't hire a cleaning person. I
SHOULD be able to do this myself, along with
everything else I do in my life."

This may have been true for the person
speaking, but it may not be true for you.

"Shoulds" are generally what someone else
has determined to be "perfect" or the "right" way.
Get a sheet of paper (any size) and write the word
"should" on it. Each time you recognize a should
that may be sabotaging you, write it on that page.

Feel free to write anywhere on that page. We are
not bound by lines or rules. You may use more than
one page This exercise is to help you recognize the
shoulds in your life that are trapping you.

Once you've filled up that page with
shoulds, burn it or rip it up, all the while thinking
that by this act you are releasing these barriers.
Continue to do this as long as shoulds keep
cropping up in your life.

EXAMPLES OF SHOULDS

I should have a better job.

I should spend more time with my children.

I should be happier.

I should talk more to my parents.

I should be more honest.

I should.......I should......I should......

CHAPTER 6

DO YOU OWN YOUR "STUFF" OR DOES YOUR "STUFF" OWN YOU?

Sitting in traffic these days, we are bombarded with the American fascination with "stuff." Bumper stickers proudly declare our commitment to the things we accumulate: "The one with the most fabric (toys, cars) at the end wins." "Shop Till You Drop."

These signs of the times read like badges of courage. More is better. Quantity wins out over quality every time.

Look around your home. Are there any clear surfaces left? Or is every nook, cranny and flat surface covered with things? Things you just picked up; things you have been collecting for years; things you have no idea how they got there. We have turned our American dream homes into makeshift warehouses for our treasures.

When describing the actually simple concept of "home," comedian George Carlin cuts right to the chase: "Your house is a place to keep your stuff while you go out and get more stuff." His words conjure up images of people (as birds) dragging back bit after bit of stuff (twigs and bark) to build a personal refuge.

Except the birds have one up on us. They abandon their nests after their function is served. We just keep adding on.

Jean, an amateur organizer helping her friend, Sandra, get organized related this story to me.

"Sandra, have you noticed that every time we clean up an area, you buy more stuff or move stuff into that area. The area you have to use remains very small!," Jean noted.

"Actually, Jean, it's funny you would bring that up. You know that I'm in therapy working through some traumas from my childhood. Well, last week I remembered that growing up in an abusive household, the only safe place I could find in my home was behind the piano. The piano was in the living room kitty-cornered between two walls. I was small enough that I could just squeeze behind the piano and no one could find me there."

"Wow, do you realize that you've recreated your childhood safe place here in your home?," asked Jean. "Look around, your stuff is placed around your house so that you have very little useable space and that useable space is in small corners."

"Now that I've worked through those old traumas, I don't need those safe spaces any more!," Sandra said. "Okay, let's start over and see what I can declutter now!!"

Why is our stuff so important to us? Psychiatrists have had field days with this particular question. Stuff buys us happiness. Stuff fills in the space a person might take up in our lives. Stuff lets us hide from our true selves.

How stuff becomes such a keystone in our lives varies with each of us. Maybe you are one of the rare birds who knows exactly why you are growing a treasure trove: You are buying comfort. You are buying security. You are buying out Wal-Mart. If you can't even begin to get a handle on your personal compulsion with things, a visit to that professional therapist might help you get to the bottom of your relationship with material goods.

Ask anyone who tragically lost everything in a fire, flood or other natural disaster what they miss most and chances are their answer will be: pictures and memorabilia.

Think about it. Have you ever met or heard of anyone who said they missed:

- the clothes that didn't fit them anymore
- the magazine articles they had cut out to read at a later time but never got around to
- the extra furniture they had bought, just in case
- gifts they had received but didn't want, need or ever like

How about you? Would the loss of the above items devastate you? Would you really miss those pants you bought on sale (what a bargain) in the hopes you could squeeze into them when you lost some weight? Would all that information in those clipped articles have made any real differences in your life? Would you ever miss those extra pieces of furniture cramping your home for years and years?

Gifts, alas, are another story. According to the dictionary, a gift is something voluntarily transferred by one person to another without compensation. If it were only that simple.

"I have a lovely house, but there's not enough storage space."

"What's in this closet in the dining room?" the organizer innocently asked.

"Those are wedding presents."

"For you?"

"Yes."

"How long have you been married?"

"Ten years."

"Have you ever used any of these gifts?"

"No, these are the duplicate gifts or gifts that don't fit our lifestyle or we just didn't like."

"Have you considered donating them or giving them to someone else?"

"I couldn't do that! Someone might ask me what I did with their gift."

"Has that happened in the last ten years?"

"No, but you never know."

There is so much emotion and guilt wrapped up in gifts, it's no wonder we take the easy way out and hold onto them forever. This kind of attitude turns these gifts into harassment, something we can live without.

Consider a new way of thinking about the gifts you receive. Think of them as something which has been given to you *with no strings* attached. If you want the gift, keep it and enjoy it. If you have no use for it or downright hate it, give it away.

Holding onto things is often an expression of our fear we will actually have a need for these items at some point. What a disaster it would be if they weren't right there ready to fill that need. The old "save it for a rainy day" concept. But for 99.9 per cent of the stuff we are holding onto, those rainy days have not and will never come.

Even if you do need these things on some distant day, will you know where to find them? Wouldn't it be easier to just go out and get what you need when you need it and reduce the stress all this clutter is producing?

CHAPTER 7

SO YOU WANT TO BE ORGANIZED... WHAT'S STOPPING YOU?

I've asked this question to every audience during the last six years of facilitating presentations. The answers I get are usually...

Time	Energy	Space
Boss	Motivation	Knowledge
Interruptions		Completions

Then I tell them the horrible truth. These are all just symptoms.

If you are not as organized as you want to be -- it's because of YOU.

One of the hardest blocks to crack in becoming organized is self-sabotage. This is not an external force we need to recognize, avoid or compromise. This is an internal, mostly hidden struggle. This struggle is between our fears, our beliefs and our desires. When they don't have a singular purpose, the fears, beliefs, desires start manipulating to get what they want. Many of us go blindly through our lives while this war rages inside, undetectable to our conscious self.

When we start to make behavioral changes, this struggle becomes more apparent. This happens because the fears, beliefs or desires believe they are under attack and must defend themselves.

Fears and beliefs are not all bad. We need them in our lives. But sometimes they conspire to keep us from having fun, making money, being in love, or acting out our desires.

Fears are a wonderful safety net. They keep us from walking in traffic or touching a hot stove.

But we've given them so much power they are also holding us back from living our dreams.

Beliefs are wonderful, too. The belief of a four-year-old not to cross the street without holding someone's hand is wonderful. The same belief in a 40-year-old (living in New York) is not only questionable, but could be dangerous.

Why would anyone (even subconsciously) sabotage his or her own needs? We humans do it all the time. Here are a few examples of self-sabotage:

- CHRONIC LATENESS
- LIVING OR WORKING IN CLUTTER
- WORKAHOLISM
- PROCRASTINATION
- PUTTING OTHERS' NEEDS FIRST

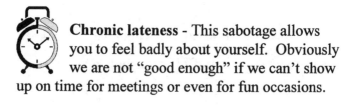 **Chronic lateness** - This sabotage allows you to feel badly about yourself. Obviously we are not "good enough" if we can't show up on time for meetings or even for fun occasions.

There's also the added self-sabotage of receiving scorn or criticism from the people who are kept waiting. They usually feel they don't have your respect.

Living or working in clutter - Clutter is different for everyone. Clutter is physical, mental, emotional and spiritual. Clutter is the material, people, ideas, fears or thoughts that are keeping us from reaching our goals. Clutter can manifest itself in too many papers or too much furniture; in too many friends or activities that keep us jumping all day. Clutter is those things that take our energy, time and money while keeping us from living the life we want!!

Workaholism - When putting all our energies to work, we're not allowing ourselves to be balanced. Balance brings about wholeness and forward movement. Balance is achieved through work, play and spirituality. When we are balanced, we are in synch with the universe and everything becomes natural and easy. By moving away from workaholism, we are allowing ourselves the freedom to do our work more easily and in less time while enjoying ourselves with others, too.

Procrastination - This can be a manifestation of our fear of failure or fear of success. We postpone doing what we love because of guilt or fear. It may also be a block due to lack of information, motivation or belief that it can be done.

For example: Every project from writing a report to gift buying has three distinct parts: beginning, momentum and completion. There are also distinct blocks which can be manifested at each stage:

- *Beginning*: You discuss the project in great detail, but have trouble actually starting.
- *Momentum:* You start projects in a snap, but get bored very quickly and let them drop without really putting energy into them.
- *Completion:* You have several (many) projects pending that just need one little item (signature, phone call, label) to complete them, but you can't bring yourself to do it.

Remember, you can have blocks in more than one area. But by being aware of your blocks, you can start to change how you operate.

Putting others' needs first - Every time we go on a plane we hear, "...if oxygen is needed, please put your mask on first, then help others with their masks." So, where did we get the idea that we need to help everyone else first, then (if there's anything left) we can help ourselves? The more we give to ourselves, the more we have to give to others. The more we help ourselves, the more help we are to others. The more we learn, the more we can teach others.

The items on this self-sabotage list are not inherently bad, of course. You may have these traits and not be self-sabotaging. But if these traits are keeping you from living your dreams, then it is sabotage.

How many of us daydream about living a different life? Instead, we live with too many if onlys -- "If only I had more time, money, energy, I could be a great..." What's holding you back? The money, the time, or you?

> *Have you ever noticed how many "really important" things get done when we are avoiding something we don't want to do?*

When we surround ourselves with material goods or people and spend our waking hours figuring out how we're going to pay for those goods or please others, we may be missing the best parts of our lives.

When we can slow down, declutter and focus, some of the questions in our heads become clearer. Such as:

- What are we doing here?
- Where do we need to be spending our energies?
- Which people do we need in our lives?
- Do we have a mission? What is it?

Then we can ask ourselves how we can implement our new way of thinking:

- What are my priorities?
- Am I living those priorities?
- What do I need to change to implement these priorities?
- What resources do I have for this change?

One caution: This is a life-changing activity. You must be aware of how you are self-sabotaging or you may fall back into an old pattern.

Do something each day to move closer to your goal!!

SECTION 2

TOOLS
FOR
CHANGE

CHAPTER 8

THE THREE KEYS TO ORGANIZING

 **DECLUTTER**

 **ORGANIZE**

 **SIMPLIFY,**
SIMPLIFY,
SIMPLIFY

# DECLUTTER:

Before decluttering, determine what clutter means to you. Clutter is anything that is keeping you from reaching your goals. It may be physical, emotional, psychological or spiritual. On a physical level, clutter may include paper, clothes, furniture, supplies, relationships, jobs, and "shoulds."

Decluttering is eliminating anything in your life that does not help you reach your goals.

The first question in decluttering is: Do I need it? The second question is: Why? The third question is: When will I need it?

ORGANIZE:

In order to be organized, you will need to design systems for the materials you are keeping. Example: Mail: Design a place for bills, letters to be read and answered, advertisements, information. Each time the mail comes in, it goes directly to that area. That way, you can always find it.

To be organized, we need to move from *I'll do it later* to *I'll put it in the designated area first, then I won't have to do it later and when I want it, I'll know where to look.* In organizing a previously unorganized area, I first collect all the materials and put them in one place. Now, even if we don't complete the organizing project that day or week, we've limited the places we need to search through.

SIMPLIFY:

Schedule your time so that you can take care of the priorities in your life. Once you have eliminated the unnecessary and designed systems for what is left, make sure there is time to keep the system maintained.

Review Chapter 12 to see how using a time diary can help you get control of your time. It's not how much time you have; it's what you do with it. Each of us, no matter how busy we are, can probably find five to ten minutes a day we can devote to decluttering, organizing or simplifying. Even if all you do is go around the office before you leave or your house before you retire and close drawers and cupboards, put away books, close files, turn off lights. These are completions and will help you move closer to your goals. The smallest steps are still forward steps.

CHAPTER 9

HELP! I'M A VISUAL

I'm a Visual. How do I organize?

Visuals need to see everything. To date, you may have been using a Camouflager's products (furniture, supplies, and equipment) to try to be organized and of course, it's not working.

It's time to rethink what you need. If you're a Visual, you need to see it. Filing cabinets work fine for Camouflagers, but what about Visuals? Try see through file cabinets (these are basically wire frames with baskets that hold hanging files). You can put them in your office (home or work) or your closet.

If you are piling papers on the floor, desk and other surfaces, try using a bookcase. It's still Visual, but it looks neater and you run less risk of knocking your piles over or having others complain about the stacks.

You can also take advantage of the new Visual organizing tools at the office supply stores. The vertical staggered file holders are a prime example of this.

Apply these same principles to any room of your house or office.

One of the biggest problems for most Visuals is how to make one item stand out. For example, you want to return a library book. How can you remember to do that if every surface in your room, office or house is covered? Two suggestions:

1. Put a post-it note on the exit door reminding you to take the book and also where you put the book.

2. Designate a staging area near the exit door that holds only those things that need to leave with you today. It's important that this staging area be kept as a primary space (or only for those things leaving that day) otherwise it will become just one more surface on which to put "stuff."

Some Visuals use the *putting the paper in front of the exit door method* so they can't miss it, but I have not found this to be as successful as the other suggestions. We are also trying to train your system that things have a place and when they are in their designated place, you are able to function more efficiently and with less frustration.

There are many levels of Visuals. There are extreme Visuals who need to see absolutely everything and there are Visuals who are closer to the middle and are able to hide things that do not need action.

It is important to determine your Visual level.

The next page illustrates an organized Visual's office. You can still see everything, but the office is neat and the papers are off the floor.

Illustration of an organized Visual's Office

CHAPTER 10

HELP! I'M A CAMOUFLAGER

Camouflagers need to have a clean environment within which to live and work. Camouflagers have always been considered the most organized people simply because others could not see their "stuff." It was hidden.

In order to be a Camouflager, you must have places to hide "stuff." Choose furniture with drawers or doors. Choose a house with lots of closets and a basement for housing "stuff." A Camouflager may even need to hide stuff from their own sight.

The key to successful camouflaging is to hide with logic. In other words, if it is a kitchen product, hide it in the kitchen or in an area which has been designed for kitchen overflow.

One of the key problems for Camouflagers is drop-by company. If they are unorganized and have not been able to keep up with the mail or papers coming into their home or office, they may have piles or stacks around. As soon as the door bell rings or a visitor is announced, they must "hide" the stuff in order to be comfortable with another person. It would be easier if there was a designated hiding area for these times. It would then be important to return to that stash and complete the decluttering process.

Remember, neat is not the same thing as organized. Being able to find it, when you need it, with the least amount of work is being organized.

There are all levels of Camouflage. It's important to recognize what your level of Camouflage is. There are extreme Camouflagers who feel having their stuff camouflaged is not sufficient. It must also be in the perfect place and neat, even if you can't see it.

Of course, you can also be a Camouflager who is closer to the middle. This would mean that anything that is finished or complete needs to be out of sight, but anything that requires an action needs to be visible.

Check on the next page for an illustration of an organized Camouflager's office.

Illustration of an organized Camouflager's office

CHAPTER 11

I LIVE (WORK) WITH AN OPPOSITE ORGANIZING STYLE

Can't live with them? Can't shoot them!

"Clean up your area!"
"Quit moving my stuff!"
"Why are you such a slob?"
"I think you're just plain lazy!"
"Are you obsessed?"

Do any of these statements sound familiar?

If so, you may be living or working with someone

with a different organizing style.

Your personal organizing style may be as

different as night and day, but those with conflicting

Visual and Camouflage styles can have successful relationships. The first step is to take the time to understand and accept each other's differences.

Let's explore those differences:

Visuals are those of us who need to see what they are looking for; that is, <u>everything</u> they might be looking for. These are the people whose homes and offices resemble background shots for the movie, "Twister." Their stuff is literally everywhere and destined to stay there. To those who do not appreciate this particular style of organizing, life with a Visual can be pretty frustrating or even frightening.

Camouflagers, on the other hand, want everything to be out of sight. Each and every item in their lives has an assigned spot and, for extreme Camouflagers, it must be in that assigned spot for them to feel right with their world. Visuals come upon this Spartan-like scene and their first comment is something like: "Come on, how can anybody live like this?" It's a question Camouflagers could ask of Visuals.

When you are in the midst of dealing with someone of the opposite organizing style, it may be difficult to believe that these two distinctly different organizing types can live in peace and harmony (in the same house or office).

The steps to achieve that harmony are:

1. Understand that although your style is different, it is the appropriate style for you. Just the fact that you can admit to having different styles is healthy for your relationship. Now that you understand each of your styles, we can start to work.

2. Learn to accept each other's organizing style and don't try to change the other person. Just because it isn't your style does not mean it is wrong or that it should be fixed. Remember the old adage: "If it ain't broke, don't fix it." Truer

words were never spoken about organizing
styles.

3. Discuss each other's organizing differences.
   Brutal honesty is the ticket here. This is not the
   time to hold back feelings about how much the
   other person's style is making you crazy. Get
   everything out in the open where you can deal
   with it.

4. Focus on the things you have in common.
   Surely there are some things you agree on. You
   may have to search deeply for them but you
   need to identify them now.

5. Compromise as a team. If both of you are
   willing to give and take, neither of you will feel
   like the only one who is making sacrifices.

6. Allow for separate space when compromise
   doesn't work. There's nothing wrong with each
   of you having a separate room or spot to call

your own. This may be one of the healthiest ways to keep the relationship intact.

7. Camouflagers can suggest the tools necessary to enhance, yet not infringe, on a Visual's style. For Visuals, putting things on bookcases still allows them to see everything, while satisfying the Camouflager's need to have things off the floor or away from eye level. Visuals can make use of see-through file cabinets and stacking trays, also acceptable to Camouflagers. Camouflagers usually have no need for new tools; most already have what they need.

8. Communicate, communicate, communicate. Keeping the lines of communication open forces issues to be resolved before irrevocable lines are drawn in the sand -- lines neither of you may be able to cross.

9. Recognize when your organizing style isn't the real issue. Using these admitted differences as a

way to cover up more serious problems in the relationship will not work long term.

10. Always remember to accept your differences and to keep the communication lines open at all times. If you can accomplish this, your relationship will move forward on a much smoother path.

Relationships help us learn and grow. Admittedly, living (or working) with someone of the opposite organizing style is a challenge. But if you can use the above strategies and make this work, think how easy all your other relationships will be.

CHAPTER 12

TIME, TIME, WHO'S GOT THE TIME?

I'm late, I'm late, for a very important date
-White Rabbit
-"Alice in Wonderland"

Feeling a bit like the White Rabbit these days? Always running but never catching up? Each of us, including the rabbit, has 24 hours in a day. No act of Congress or of any other earthly power can change that. We can change, though, what we do with that time.

The first step in getting more time in your life is becoming aware of how you are now spending your time.

A time diary can help you discover why you feel you're being cheated out of your share of precious time. This kind of diary can be used for a month, a week, or for as little as two days. No matter how long you use it to record activities, you'll begin to pick up patterns about how you use your time.

TIME	Personal hygiene	Exercise	Work projects	Recrea-tion
6 AM				
7 AM				
8 AM				

The time diary breaks down your day into one-hour increments, making it easy to record where your time goes. To make a diary, simply draw a chart with the hours of the day written on the left-hand side. List the tasks you must do (personal hygiene, exercise, work projects, commuting, recreation, etc.) across the top. Whenever you spend time doing something within those categories, place a check mark in the appropriate box.

This diary will help you determine whether you are a Focused worker or a Grazer. Remember, a Focused worker is someone who works on one project and one project only until it is completed. This will become apparent because only one of your projects has check marks in its block.

If, however, you have made check marks in the blocks under several different projects, you are most likely a Grazer, a worker who is less structured.

Both of these ways of working are fine, but it is important to know which one you use. (See Chapter 4 for more information.)

Focused workers function best with a structured time schedule: "from 9 to 10 a.m., I will return phone calls; from 10 to 11 a.m., I will work on the Grason project..." and so on.

Grazers, on the other hand, hate that kind of structure. They prefer a weekly or even monthly goal to an hourly one. One of the simple ways to help Grazers complete projects (because this may be an issue for them) is to make a chart listing all their projects. Each time a task is done for a project or progress is made toward completion, an "x" is jotted down next to that project name. This allows Grazers to see what kind of progress is being made on each of their projects, prompting them to spend more time on those which are not moving forward.

PROJECT	COMPLETED
Write my book	XX
Organize my clothes	X
Write my mother	XXXX
Schedule a party	

I walked in to find my client nervously pacing back and forth. "What's wrong?," I asked.

"I don't have time to get organized or even be disorganized. I don't even have time for this meeting. I should have canceled."

"Well, I'm here now," I said. "Why don't we try to work through this. What seems to be the problem with your time?"

"I don't have enough of it to complete my work," my client replied.

I got out my legal pad and said, "Let's write down what you have to do this week."

"First off, I'm scheduled to be in the Fourth of July parade on Friday, so that day is totally shot," he said.

"When and where do you need to meet for the parade?," I asked

"Noon, at the park two miles from here."

"How long will the parade last?"

"One hour."

"Is there anything planned afterwards?"

"No, everyone will be going off on their own afterwards."

"Why is Friday totally shot if the park is only two miles from here and it's only going to take one hour for the parade?"

"Well, when you put it that way, I guess it seems pretty silly."

"Not at all." I said, "But you can see how the perception of time changes how we make use of the time we do have. You would have just wasted Friday because your perception was that it was lost anyway. Now you can use it productively. Let's go through the rest of the week and set goals and schedules."

"Great idea, now that I have Friday back, I won't have any problems at all with my deadlines. Thanks."

If this type of time management strikes you as a little abstract, it really isn't. What time management really comes down to, bottom-line, is asking the question: Looking back over the past week, how do you feel about the time you spent? Do you feel a sense of accomplishment? Do you feel you were running in place, dodging arrows all week and you didn't do any of what you really wanted to do? Or do you feel happy about what you've done and look forward to the next week?

Regardless of what your work habits are, you can feel good about how you spend your time each week. If you don't, it could be that you are not spending your time the way you really want to.

How many times last week did you say, "I don't have time to do that?" Is that really true (be honest) or was "that" just not a high enough priority for you or not worth the scheduling changes it required? (The next time someone tells you "I don't have time to do that," what they are really saying is "that's not a high enough priority for me.")

Truth is, you set your own schedule even if you feel if you don't. Since you are responsible for how your time is spent, take the time you need to set your priorities, and then make sure you leave time in your schedule for those things that are important to you.

If you choose not to set priorities and goals for yourself, others will be glad to set them for you, something you really don't want. When other people begin telling you what to do with your time, it's only natural to feel like your life is out of control. The reality is that *your* life is out of *your* control.

Naturally, there are times when we willingly place control for our time in someone else's hands. But if we do that too often, the feelings of being out-of-control and overwhelmed begin to take over.

To rid yourself of those negative feelings, begin to set your own priorities now and stick to them as best you can. If these priorities are based on your personal goals, you'll find you can achieve more in your life than you ever thought.

Decide today where you want to be in your life and what your priorities must be to get there. You'll not only accomplish your goals, you'll be able to look back over each week with feelings of joy and peace of mind, the worthiest goals of all.

CHAPTER 13

CREATE YOUR OWN CLUTTER-FREE ZONES

So, you're living in a cluttered environment! What to do? Start small.

Pick one area to create as a clutter-free zone. As a suggestion, pick a small area. If you have no small areas, choose one corner of a room. This may mean that you just pick everything up from that corner and move it into another room. That's okay. Even better would be to declutter it, but one step at a time. This is a process.

Now, designate a use for the zone and start using it. At the end of the day, check the "zone" to make sure it's clutter-free.

Once you've lived with this zone for a while (maybe a week) and are comfortable in the space and convinced that you can keep it clutter-free, choose a second space.

Once you've created two clutter-free zones, add in 15 minutes per day of decluttering.

Set a timer for 15 minutes and just declutter (eliminate unnecessary items) until the timer rings. Now some would say that this process is too slow. But I say that it is progress. Also, it is done in such small increments that it may not bring up your fears. If you continually declutter for 15 minutes, you will start to see a difference in your environment.

Continue this process, decluttering and creating clutter-free zones. Toward the end, you may end up with one area which is holding the stuff from all the other areas.

Now, we get to work. During your process of designating uses for the clutter-free zones and decluttering, you may have gotten a better idea of what you need to keep and what you can eliminate.

There are several options at this point.

1. You can move all the stuff into a warehouse and eliminate one box a week until it is all gone.
2. You can leave it in the room and pull out one box a week to eliminate.
3. There's always the option, of course, of hiring a professional organizer if you can't complete this project on your own or in the time frame you need.
4. You could also have a decluttering party. Invite all your friends over to take what they want from you as long as they help you throw out or donate what no one wants. Be careful not to include friends who are also having difficulty decluttering; you'll only be adding to their problems.

Some people, once they've created the clutter-free zones, are loath to bring any clutter into those areas ever again. You'll decide which option is best for you.

CHAPTER 14

BREAK THE CLUTTER HABIT

If you are living in a cluttered environment, you are training your system to ignore the clutter around you. If you are continually ignoring the clutter, you may also be ignoring or oblivious to the opportunities around you.

Breaking the clutter habit calls for awareness, decluttering and completions.

Awareness can be achieved by setting a timer for five minutes each day and really looking at your environment. Look at it with no judgement and no rationalizations, but really look at it. Look at it as though you're in real estate and have no attachment to the property. Then take a moment to decide whether this is the environment that is most conducive to your good physical and mental health.

If not, start making changes -- small changes -- but changes no less.

Decluttering can be achieved by setting a timer for 15 minutes every day and just decluttering. Always start with the easy stuff. When we start with the harder stuff, we just invite our self-sabotage and fears to kick it. Start with easy stuff -- like junk mail, old newspapers, old magazines. When you hit a wall, back up and go in another direction. I'm sure you can keep finding stuff to declutter for 15 minutes.

> *I declutter ever single day for at least five minutes. I happen to be a minimalist and a professional organizer so my friends don't understand how I can declutter every day. There is always another space or area that can be cleaned out. I get mail every day. I change my mind about clothes, about papers that I've kept, about files, even coupons that have expired. There always seems to be something that can be decluttered. I keep decluttering every day to keep in the*

habit, but also to keep the opportunities and abundance flowing. (See Chapter 23 for more information).

Completions can also be done with a timer. Before you retire each night (or before you leave work), set your timer for five minutes and go around doing completions. This may be as simple as:

- closing all the drawers and doors.
- returning books that were pulled out during the day.
- turning off all the lights.
- returning furniture to its designated place.
- putting files or papers away that were pulled out.

Any small completion is still a completion.

Five minutes or fifteen minutes may not seem like long enough to make a real difference in your environment, but your system is learning to trust awareness, decluttering and completions.

Once your system is more comfortable with these concepts and understands they are helpful, not harmful to you, the organizing path will become easier.

CHAPTER 15

MOTIVATION – CARROT OR STICK: WHICH WILL WORK FOR YOU?

You've established your goals, you've determined your motivation, now how do you keep the momentum going?

Remember the story of the horse that runs as fast as he can to catch a carrot dangling from a stick in front of his nose? Well, humans respond as well to the "carrot" or reward as any horse ever could. And just as many of us are more inclined to respond to the "stick" or some form of denial or punishment to motivate us.

Motivation is a key component to behavioral modification. If earning a reward (a night on the town) will motivate us to get organized, then so be it. If, on the other hand, a stronger motivation for you is to lose the reward (and give the money you would have spent on the night on the town to charity), then so be that, too.

To begin any organizational project, break it down into small (sometimes tiny) components which will allow you to see progress, always the best motivator.

This chart shows the three ways people usually get organized:

1. Take a two-week vacation and spend every minute decluttering and organizing.
2. Take one Saturday a month and spend every minute decluttering and organizing.
3. Take 15 minutes a day.

Choice #1 is a sure organizing killer. Very few people would enjoy this (unless of course you're working with a professional organizer!)

Choice #2 could be detrimental unless handled properly.

Choice #3 is primarily for maintenance. If you have been avoiding decluttering or organizing, though, this may be a way to get it done. Make a list of projects; break them down into components that can be completed in a 15-minute increment. Set your timer for 15 minutes and organize. This may take a little longer, but it will get the job done. You will also have decluttering and completion accomplishments every day, which will help you become more productive at it.

Here's a tip to get you started organizing:

- List your organizational projects. Then code them by jobs you would enjoy doing and those you would rather avoid. Here's where the carrot comes in. There are three different ways to use the carrot. You may choose any of these.

1. Accomplish one project you will enjoy and then one project you want to avoid. You've gotten your reward first.

2. Do one project you want to avoid followed by one you are looking forward to. In this way, you can congratulate yourself for doing the work by receiving a reward.

3. Schedule time (i.e. one hour) for organizing followed by a 15 to 30 minute break when you do something you enjoy (walk, dance, read, eat, etc.) Some people think this is not productive, but I've found when people focus for a short time with some kind of reward following it, they achieve more than if they have tried to make themselves focus on the project for a whole day (or even half day).

SECTION 3

IDEAS FOR SPECIFIC AREAS

CHAPTER 16

SETTING UP A WORK AREA

"How many of you have an office in your home?," asked the facilitator.

Three hands went up.

"How many of you pay your bills at home?"

All hands went up.

"How many of you track your insurance and financial papers at home?"

All hands went up.

"Now, how many of you have an office in your home?"

All hands went up with a few nods and sheepish grins.

Every one of us has an office. It may be in the workplace, it may be in our car, it may be in the basement, kitchen or spare bedroom, but every one of us has an office.

An office is simply a space where you can pay bills, keep important papers, write letters, track information and make decisions.

And with the proliferation of home-based and small businesses, we've seen an increase of business offices at home.

The information in this chapter can be used for an office at a company, a home-based business, a small business, or an office just for home use. It can also be used for students, homemakers and sales people on the road.

When you have never had an office, how do you set up a workspace to be organized and efficient?

First, let's talk about how to divide the three kinds of space by function:

1. Primary -- the space where you will be doing most of the work. This would be the area for things that are needed on a daily or weekly basis.

   - In your car, this would be the passenger seat.
   - In your office this would be the top of your desk.
   - For a Visual, this would be the top of your desk.
   - For a Camouflager, this would be the desk drawers that you can easily reach from a sitting position.

2. Secondary -- an area close to the primary area. This would be for things needed every other week or monthly or even quarterly.

   - In your car, this would be the trunk.
   - In your office, this would be the file cabinet or bookcase away from your desk.

- For a Visual, this would be a bookcase away from your desk.
- For a Camouflager, this would be a file cabinet or closet away from your desk.

3. Tertiary -- an area farther away from the primary area. It could be off the premises or a garage, basement or storage area. It would be for those things that need to be kept, but would not frequently be looked at, if ever.

- For your car, this would be things left at the office or home.
- For your office, this would be a storage area, basement or secretary's area.
- For a Visual and Camouflager, this would be another room or storage area.

When setting up your workspace, it is important to first understand what you will be doing in that area and what equipment and supplies you will need.

Each of us has finite space in which to do our work. How are you using yours?

CHAPTER 17

 **SETTING UP A FILING SYSTEM**

Filing systems are extensions of our minds. This can be a scary thought. Some of us have conflicting ideas and goals (sometimes called committees in our minds) making it difficult to make decisions. However, even with committees, decisions can be made eventually.

To create a filing system, we first want to decide what we want to achieve with it. In other words, what do we want the filing system to do for us?

In most cases, we want the filing systems to hold the information that we don't want to keep in our minds. We want the filing systems to hold the papers and materials that we will need in order to prove that something happened or that we own something. We want the filing system to allow us to do our work without worrying about where the papers are and how we're going to retrieve them.

There are a myriad of ways to set up filing systems. You can check any of the organizing books to learn how to set up alphabetical, numerical or subject filing systems. You can learn how to set up computer filing programs or use index cards to keep track.

My primary question is: Will the filing system you choose work for you? Remember, being organized means you can find what you need, when you need it, with the least amount of work.

For filing systems, this means:

89

1. If you are proficient at the computer and find it easier to find stuff on it, put your filing system on the computer.
2. If you work better by dates, set your filing system up that way.
3. If you work better by subject, set your filing system up that way.

Your filing system does not have to be the same for all items. You can have some by date -- such as paid bills or things to do. You can have some by subject -- such as resources or basic home information. You can have some alphabetical -- such as by client or kids' names.

This filing system should reflect you and the way you work. Stop and think about where you would look for items when you need them. Then use this information to set up your personal, efficient filing system.

Question to organizer during presentation: "I keep looking for the plumber's telephone number under "p" for plumber. Should I move his telephone number there?"

"Yes, the first place you look for an item is probably the best place to keep it."

Always keep this concept in mind when you set up your filing system.

CHAPTER 18

CLOSETS

Closets are places to store things you want to get to. It would therefore be important to know which things you want to get to and how often you need them.

One way to decide how to use your closets is to sketch out your home, including closets. Now, think about how each room is to be used. List the items you will want to use in that room. For example: you would want food items and supplies near your kitchen.

Now look at the items you have listed, and break them down into primary, secondary and tertiary.

- Primary -- Things you need on a daily or weekly basis.
- Secondary -- Things you need on a monthly or quarterly basis.
- Tertiary -- Things you need on a yearly basis.

Primary items should be within easy reach of where you will be using them. Secondary items should be within easy walking distance from where you will be using them. Tertiary items should be stored where you can get to them, but should not take up primary or secondary space.

For example, if you always get dressed in the bathroom on the main floor, why are your clothes kept on the third floor? You might want to rethink either where you get dressed or where you keep your clothes.

When setting up closets, one of the first questions people ask is: What will fit in here? My first question is: What would be of most use in here? What is this closet closest to?

Just because a contractor has named a closet does not mean it has to be used for that purpose. For example, if a linen closet happens to be closer to the kitchen than the pantry, I would use the linen closet for a pantry, because it is my area and it works best for me.

Being organized means making things easy for yourself so you can focus your time and energy on what you really want to do.

Set up your closets so they work for you, not so they fit someone else's idea of how a house should be set up.

CHAPTER 19

 CLOTHES

When organizing clothes, it is important to recognize that there are many emotional and psychological attachments to them. Clothes are what we put on to tell others what and who we are, but they may or may not be a true reflection of what we want the world to see. When dealing with organizing clothes, it is important to keep this focus in mind.

When decluttering clothes, start with the easiest ones to make decisions on first. Don't let the cost of an item interfere with your decision to keep or declutter it.

Begin with:

1. Clothes that don't fit and have no possibility of fitting.
2. Clothes that are too big right now if you are losing weight. This will encourage you to continue with your healthier lifestyle.
3. Maternity clothes if you are not planning on having more children.
4. Fad clothing that you won't wear today or in the very near future. If the fad does come back, it's unlikely you will wear these items anyway and you'll just worry about how much money you've wasted.
5. Shoes that are worn out or never fit right.
6. Clothes that were bought for a specific lifestyle or sport that you no longer do.

Once you've eliminated the easy items, we'll start on the ones that seem harder:

1. Gifts from others that didn't fit, you didn't like or just don't reflect you.

2. Clothes that didn't fit right in the first place and still don't.
3. Clothes that fit, but you don't like for some reason.
4. Clothes that fit, but you don't like the statement they make about you.
5. Clothes that fit, but you don't want to wear that kind of material any more.
6. Clothes that fit, but you feel uncomfortable in them for some reason.

It is not necessary to do this decluttering all at once. In fact, it is probably easier on the system to set a timer for 15 to 30 minutes and start at one end of a closet. When the timer sounds, put a hanger with a ribbon wound around it where you stopped, so that the next time you have 15 to 30 minutes you can start from that point and move forward.

It would also be beneficial if you set up boxes for charity, resale, garbage, and repair. Mark these boxes and keep them handy for the decluttering. When they become full, bag them up and deliver them to the appropriate areas.

Some people think they can just make piles of clothes and will remember what their intentions were. This fails more than it works. By having the boxes always available, you have eliminated the possibility of:

1. Getting interrupted and not being able to complete the decluttering.
2. Running out of time and just dumping all the clothes together to deal with later.
3. Forgetting what the different piles represent and having to make the decisions a second or third time.

When dealing with clothes, it is important to take into consideration our emotional picture of ourselves and how we feel about our bodies. When you open your main closet every morning, what emotional picture do you get?

"I received four compliments when wearing the blue dress yesterday that my sister had sent me. It is just my color, my size, it shows off my assets, but I still don't feel good in it. Looking back at the last two years, I realize that I've worn it about two times. I usually wear clothes that get me compliments more often than that. I tried to figure out why I didn't feel good in it. I thought back to when I received it from my sister. My sister and I are the same size and trade clothes a lot. I called her about two years ago and asked if she had any clothes she wasn't wearing because I needed a pick-me-up. She said no, she had sent her clothes to my other sister. I told her that things were going badly. I was in the midst of a divorce, in the midle of winter in Pittsburgh and money was really tight. I was feeling particularly boxed in. Two days later, I received a box from my sister with this dress. The moment I opened the box, I cried. I immediately sensed that she had felt sorry for me and was

99

sending me a dress that she needed
because she felt I needed it more.
Now, whenever I put on that dress, I
feel that she feels sorry for me. I'm
going to send it back to her. I don't
want that energy around me any
more."

In your primary closet, keep only those
clothes that you can fit into, that make you feel good
about yourself and that are the appropriate season.
If you cannot keep the other items in another closet,
at least keep them to the sides of the closet, where
you will not need to see them every moment.

Most of us don't need to start out the day
feeling bad about ourselves. Most of us would be
better served by feeling good about ourselves at the
start of every day.

When holding onto "good" clothes that are
not your size or need at the moment, you are
keeping others from using those clothes. Every
time I think this, I realize that by hoarding my

clothes – just in case – I am keeping someone else from using them -- today.

I believe when and if I need clothes like this again I will run into someone else who is decluttering those items and I can get them then. By keeping the cycle moving, we insure this happening.

CHAPTER 20

KITCHENS

Many kitchens are designed to be the family's focal point. In keeping with your family's lifestyle, note the different ways you use your particular kitchen.

In the kitchen, as in the other areas of our homes, we have finite space. The most used space is the counter top. To be organized, you need to focus on your kitchen space just as we have the other spaces of your home.

Let's review the use of the space:

1. Primary -- The primary space in your kitchen is the counter top. The counter tops should hold only those items that are used on a daily basis or

that would be difficult to take out and put away often.

2. Secondary -- The secondary areas in kitchens would be inside cupboards or the pantry. These areas would be for items that are used on a weekly or monthly basis and for dishes and glasses that are used daily, but would not be appropriate for the counter tops.

3. Tertiary -- The tertiary areas in kitchens would be the basement or attic. These areas would be for items used seasonally or once a year.

When designing a kitchen, one of the first suggestions I hear is "Where is this supposed to go?" Don't get stuck on how you think others would set up your kitchen.

I change the question to, "Where would this be needed?" "How often?"

When my kitchen is organized, I can reach out for what I need without really thinking about it.

It has moved into the automatic response. This allows me to think about the recipe, about other things I am cooking, about the party I'm planning, about other things that are happening in my life. I don't need to expend energy thinking about where a bowl is, or where the measuring cup is.

"I can't use this kitchen at all. Every time I reach for something it's on the other side of the room. What can I do?"

We were standing in Cindy's country kitchen, which happened to be as large as my living room. The kitchen also had a large table sitting in the middle of it, which made moving from one side of the room to the other difficult.

"Tell me what items you use when you cook."

Cindy started telling me what she uses and I took notes. When she had finished, I asked, "Cindy, you didn't mention the microwave oven. Do you use that often?"

"No, I hardly use it at all."

"Let's move it to the seldom used side of the kitchen."

"It also hurts my back to bend down to get the pans from the bottom shelf."

"Then, let's move the pans up to eye level."

"We can do that?" Cindy asked.

"Absolutely. It's your kitchen. We can do anything we want. In fact, let's go through this list and move everything you use over to the most often used side and everything you don't use over to the least often used side of the kitchen."

Two weeks later I called to check on Cindy's progress.

"Absolutely great, I can cook an entire dinner just in this one little area and I'm not running all over the kitchen trying to find things or get things. It's working great!"

When I set up a kitchen, the first thing I suggest is that you label the cupboards and drawers so that everyone in the house knows where everything lives. That way, it has a better change of getting back where it belongs.

The first couple of weeks in a newly organized kitchen are the crucial weeks. This is the time when we are adjusting to our new setup.

When you are setting up a new kitchen or reorganizing an old one, here are the questions you could ask:

1. Where will I use this item?
2. How often will I use this item?
3. What will I be doing when I use this item?

Here are some examples:

- When standing at the sink, where would you reach for a glass?

- When standing at the stove, where would you reach for a utensil?

- When setting the table, where would you reach for the dishes, tableware, napkins, placemats, etc.?

- When cooking at the stove, where would you reach for a pot?

- When putting leftovers away, where would you reach for a container?

"I cannot use this kitchen. I can't find anything," Helen lamented.

I'd heard this before, so I was ready. "Helen, while we're in the kitchen, let's do an experiment. Close your eyes. Now, you're going to make pancakes. Where would you reach for the mixing bowl?"

Helen reached up and to the right.

"Now, where would you reach for the spoon to stir it?"

Helen reached down and to the left.

"Now, where would you reach for the pancake mix?"

Helen reached up and to the left.

"I marked on the diagram where you reached for the different items. Now, let's start setting up the kitchen. We'll use some other role playing as we need to."

"Thanks," Helen said. "I feel more organized already."

How do you and your family use your kitchen? What is the best way for you to set it up? Don't forget that as your family grows, your organizational needs will change. When the kids are small, you will need to childproof the kitchen and move snacks out of their reach. When they are older, you will need to move the snacks and breakables even further away from their reach. And when they reach teenage years, forget it, they can reach anything you can reach.

If you set up your kitchen according to how you use it, making these changes will be easier than you even thought.

CHAPTER 21

GARAGES/ BASEMENTS

Garages and basements have long been designated as the place to dump anything you can't make a decision about.

I feel it is really a disservice to have large basements that can be cluttered and cluttered, because when they become too cluttered there is so much to get rid of, most people don't know where to begin to declutter so they never do.

Basements and garages are great places to *temporarily* house stuff until it can be used or discarded. The important word here is temporarily.

What are some items that are perfect for storing in the basement or garage?

1. Baby furniture between children
2. Seasonal furniture
3. Yard supplies and equipment
4. Tertiary items
5. Memorabilia

The basement and garage can also be used as a temporary housing area for stuff until you make a final decision, such as:

- Clothing on its way to flea markets or charities
- Furniture on its way to flea markets or charities
- Trash on its way out of the house
- Recyclables on their way out of the house

For other things that find their way into your garage or basement, it is important that time be set aside on a monthly or quarterly basis to declutter. If these areas are left unattended for very long, they seem to multiply.

One of the easiest ways to stay in control of the garage or basement is to schedule time before each week's trash day to declutter the basement or garage. This may manifest itself in only one box from those areas being eliminated. But that's one less box to step over.

Take control of your basement and garage and it will be reflected in all your rooms.

SECTION 4

SIMPLIFY
AND
LIVE
YOUR LIFE

CHAPTER 22

SIMPLIFY

Growing up, I felt that summer vacations (three months) were way too short to get everything accomplished I wanted to do. I needed to catch up on fun reading and do all the craft work I loved, not to mention playing in the woods and relaxing in the sun.

After a few years of working, I recognized that summer vacations (two weeks) were way too short to get everything accomplished I wanted to do. After all, I needed to rejuvenate from the last year and read all the fun books I'd missed and see all the movies I'd been too busy to see and maybe relax for a day or two or go to a vacation resort.

Now that I've been an entrepreneur for six years, I've recognized that every day is a vacation day. I can do just exactly what I want to do and when. I didn't realize I had that option all along. Now I know there are choices that we make and consequences for those choices.

I now choose some days to go rollerblading during the day. (It's really more fun during the day when the sun is shining and everyone else is working.) I know that my work has to get done, but I can choose when to do it.

I've finally realized that in order to be happy all the time, I need the flexibility to choose when I do work and when I play. And I also want the flexibility to play when I'm working.

I've also recognized that not everyone wants the flexibility or the stress that goes along with being a business owner or entrepreneur. But, we **can** build flexibility into our lives within the constraints of our jobs and lives.

To simplify is similar to decluttering in that we are eliminating things from our schedule that are not "feeding" us. To simplify is to prioritize how we are using our time. To simplify is to understand what we (individually) need in order to be happy and fulfill our goals.

Simplification comes in many forms.

- Physical
- Emotional
- Mental
- Spiritual

To simplify in the physical world, declutter. Then each time you want to bring something back into your environment, ask these questions: Will this make me happy? Will this help me reach my goals?

One way to simplify in the physical world is for each new thing you bring into your environment, you release one thing from your environment. If you want to simplify more quickly, each time you bring one new thing in, release two things. Or each time you bring one new thing in, release five things. You decide how quickly you want to simplify. The more stuff you hold onto, the more stuff you are responsible for.

To simplify in the mental world means to keep the clutter in our minds to a minimum. Too many times we feel we need to make decisions in all parts of our lives at this moment. And since most of us can't make that many decisions at once (especially when we can't determine the consequences or outcome), we do nothing. Which, of course, keeps our mental clutter high. In order to mentally simplify, keep the needed decisions to a minimum. This means to limit your worries or decisions to the ones pertinent at this moment.

> *"Jane, I can't decide what to do. I want to change my life. I want a divorce. I want a new career. I want to live somewhere else. I want new relationships. I want to eat differently..."*

"Whoa! Slow down. That's a lot to decide in the moment. Let's take one decision at a time. Now, do you want to eat meat today?"

"No."

"Good. You've made one decision. Now, we can move on to the next one."

The only thing you have to decide today is if you want tomorrow to be like today. If you do, fine. If you don't, make one small decision to change. The decision might be to spend five minutes decluttering or five minutes praying or meditating. You've now done something toward changing tomorrow.

To simplify emotionally, you must be willing to allow your emotions to come out honestly. When we are not honestly aware of our emotions, about how we feel about things, how can we start to simplify? If you are angry, admit it and start asking yourself why you are angry and what you can do about it. The only true control we have

in the world is how we respond. If we are run by
our emotions, then we will never be in control.

> *Nationally known author*
> *Wayne Dyer during one of his*
> *presentations:*
>
> *Here we have an orange.*
> *Looks like an ordinary orange.*
> *When you squeeze an orange, what*
> *do you get?*
>
> *Orange Juice.*
>
> *When you squeeze an*
> *orange that hasn't had enough*
> *sleep, what do you get?*
>
> *Orange Juice.*
>
> *When you squeeze an*
> *orange that is worried about its job,*
> *what do you get?*
>
> *Orange Juice.*
>
> *When someone squeezes*
> *you, what do they get?*
>
> *They get what is inside you.*

Whenever I find myself over-reacting and
spewing out something other than my best, I think
about this orange juice story and stop. I then decide

that it may be time to discover why I'm reacting in that way. If you are stressed out and reacting in ways you're not proud of, you may want to simplify your life to eliminate some of the stress.

To simplify spiritually, you may have to eliminate all those things, ideas, and people that are holding you back from living the spiritual life you wish for. None of us knows how much time we have on the planet. If we spend that time wishing to be someone else, then we are wasting that time.

If we spend that time trying to be the person we wish to be, then we are at least moving in the direction of our goal.

If I am not for myself, who is for me?
And when I am for myself, what am I?
If not now, when?

-- Hillel
-- "The Wisdom of the Fathers"

CHAPTER 23

DECLUTTER AND
ABUNDANCE: $$
WHAT'S THE
TRICK?

"But what if I need it tomorrow?"

Maybe you believe God or the universe won't provide you with what you need when you need it, so you've decided to hold onto everything.

> *"The last time I gave something away, I discovered a use for it the very next day," a workshop participant said.*
>
> *"How long had you held onto it with no apparent use before you decluttered it?," asked the organizer."*
>
> *"Six years."*
>
> *"So, six years of seeing the object didn't excite your creativity,*

but giving it away did. Could you
focus the creativity you now have in
a direction that uses some of the
other items you're not using? Or
maybe give those items away and
see how creative you can become."

Try looking at your possessions with this different viewpoint. One that believes you will always receive everything you need.

What would happen if you released those old, unused, unwanted items (and often this includes relationships we hold onto in case we never develop new ones)? Our unneeded clutter will find its rightful place in society. It may be just the thing that someone else needs.

"I'm miserable. I'm out of
work, it's winter, I've got a cold
and I think I'm going through the
'change.' My life stinks. It can't
get any worse."

I'd been hearing this lament
every day for about three weeks
when I brought up "decluttering."

"Well, I don't see how it can

help, but it can't hurt either," she said. "Okay, I'll declutter the attic. It hasn't been touched in seven years, except to push more stuff up there."

I heard nothing for three days then:

"Hey, I decluttered the attic. It's totally empty. I donated, trashed or started using the stuff that was there. That wasn't too bad. In fact, I think I lost weight. It must be from going up and down the steps. I feel much lighter."

Day Four: "You won't believe this, I just got a call offering me a part-time job. I don't start for two weeks and I enjoyed the feeling of decluttering the attic so much, I think I'll declutter the bedroom."

Day Seven: "I decluttered the bedroom. I really think I lost weight. I feel much lighter. It must be all those steps."

Day Eight: "You won't believe it. I just got offered another part-time job. Together, I'm working less hours and making more money. But I don't start for another week so I think I'll declutter the hall closet."

Day Ten: "I decluttered the hall closet. And I really feel lighter, though I didn't do much running up and down the steps this time. It must be something else that makes me feel lighter. But it was really good to clean out that junk."

Day Eleven: "You really won't believe this. I just got a call telling me that I won a contest. Let's see: I decluttered the attic...I got a job. I decluttered the bedroom...I got a job. I decluttered the hall closet...I won a contest. Wow, this decluttering really works! But, I'm not taking out the garbage or throwing anything else out until I adjust to the fact that my life is wonderful...then I'm starting downstairs."

This decluttering can also provide the space we need for our new abundance -- new relationships, money, clarity on our path, time, energy, etc.

In business, if we want new clients, we must have room for them. We must have the time to provide them with what they need, to have the administrative time to serve them, and to follow up on their progress. When we don't have room for new clients, how can we continue to hope that we'll still get them?

Making room in our lives for our new abundance is a wonderful step towards the future you've wanted. If the concept of releasing the old unwanted items is scary, try releasing small items first and watch what happens. I think you're in for a terrific surprise.

CHAPTER 24

EXTRA TIME, ENERGY AND MONEY

If you are organized, I believe you will have more time, energy and money. Let me explain:

If you are currently searching for things you need in your life, being organized will eliminate that -- freeing up time.

If you are frustrated by not being able to find things, being organized will eliminate that drain on your energy -- giving you more energy.

If you have organized and you're spending less time and energy finding your stuff, then you can spend that time and energy making money.

Also, if you know where your stuff is, then you won't have to run out and buy more, saving even more time and money.

There are two things to consider when dealing with extra time, energy and money.

The first is how to free yourself from the fear of the unknown. If you have extra time, energy and money, what will you do with it? Will you be paralyzed by indecision on what to do next, or will you use that time, energy and money to move closer to your goals?

The second is the need to set some quantifiable benchmarks to help you recognize that you are making progress.

On the first point, only you can decide if you can successfully deal with this fear. How much do you hate where you are now and how much do you want to change?

To help avoid the fear of what to do next, make a listing of all those things you've been wanting to do, but didn't have the time, energy or money. Now put it in a safe place. Better yet, put it in a place where you can see it. This will help you keep moving towards being organized. This too can be a motivator.

On the second point, once you decide that you want to be more organized and benefit by having more time, energy and money, it is imperative that you set some quantifiable motivators.

Peace of mind as a motivator for behavioral modification is laudable but unrealistic. Peace of mind is a subjective feeling, which can be changed by external or internal forces not relating to organizing. If you decide that you want to spend more time with your family however, you can quantify that simply by checking your calendar to see if you are accomplishing that goal. It is beneficial to have a goal to work toward and benchmarks to mark your progress.

Behavioral modification is simply changing the way we work or our patterns. In order to create a new pattern, we must first recognize the old pattern, accept that we are using that pattern and find a motivation to change the pattern. Review chapter 12 to discover your current patterns. In several studies, it has been reported that if you can do a new pattern 21 times consecutively, it will then become your new pattern.

Decide whether you want to remain where you are or whether you want to change. If you want to change, do one small thing today to move closer to your goals.

CONCLUSION

Being organized means **being able to find what you need, when you need it, with the least amount of work involved.**

Being organized is a step toward living the life you want. When you are ready to make the first steps, go. When you are conflicted about moving forward, make tiny, baby steps. When you are sure that the time is not right to make changes, stay where you are. But even if the time is not right to make changes, that doesn't mean you can't be thinking, reading or planning for them.

If your life is just exactly the way you want it, congratulations. Following some of the suggestions in this book will allow you to have even more time enjoying your life.

The whole idea behind Organized Chaos is to help you recognize how you are living and decide whether that's the way you want to live or not.

There is no judgement connected to being organized. Being organized just frees you up to live the life you love. We all move at our own pace and organize the way that is best for us.

There is never an end to organizing. Organizing is a consistent on-going process which is flexible enough to change when your needs change. Some people believe once you set up your system, it never changes. How can that be? We are in constant flux. Our lives are constantly changing. And even if they aren't changing very fast, they change as we move through our life cycles. Enjoy the process. Let it work for you.

I sincerely wish for you a wonderful life full of changes and growth.

About the Author

The key to being organized

Is to understand yourself

Sylvia Jessy

Sylvia has been organizing others since the age of four (according to her mother) and for her entire professional career. After working as an office manager in 14 different industries over 20 years, friends began asking her to help them streamline their lives. In 1992, the business blossomed into Organized Chaos, a company offering professional organizing services, classes and individual coaching.

"A professional organizer is part psychologist, part coach and part teacher," Sylvia says. "There are so many misconceptions about organization. People think getting organized has to be difficult or that it means being neat and having a clean desk. That's just not true. Being organized means having more of the things you value -- time, energy and money. It means having the freedom to spend time on your personal priorities."

Sylvia first helps clients recognize their unique organizing style. Then she tailors a system to their needs and personality. Organizing services can range from a single visit to a year's worth of consultations.

Recently, Sylvia has been asked to help people simplify their lives, weed out the unimportant and set personal priorities. "Voluntary simplicity seems to be very attractive to most people right now. Their lives and commitments overwhelm them. They want to simplify their lives and have more time to enjoy their top priorities."

Originally from Virginia, Sylvia now resides in Pittsburgh and travels throughout the country presenting workshops and as a motivational speaker.

WHAT IS AVAILABLE FROM
ORGANIZED CHAOS?

We are continually adding to our available books, workbooks, products, and teaching materials.

To find out what's new:

Call (412) 362-0793

Outside PA (888)-TO-CHAOS

E-mail – OrganizedChaos@Juno.com

SJessy@aol.com

Fax – (412)-362-4927

Organized Chaos
associates are available for:
Coaching
Consultations
Workshops
Seminars
Keynote Speeches